THE

TRAEGER GRILL &

SMOKER

COOKBOOK

Master the Art of Grilling with Your

Traeger Grill and Smoker 50

Mouthwatering Recipes

By

American Chef's Table

and a Committee of Publishers and Associations.

In no way is it legal to reproduce, duplicate, or transmit any part of this document in either electronic means or in printed format. Recording of this publication is strictly prohibited and any storage of this document is not allowed unless with written permission from the publisher.

The information provided herein is stated to be truthful and consistent, in that any liability, in terms of inattention or otherwise, by any usage or abuse of any policies, processes, or Instructions contained within is the solitary and utter responsibility of the recipient reader. Under no circumstances will any legal responsibility or blame be held against the publisher for any reparation, damages, or monetary loss due to the information herein, either directly or indirectly.

Respective authors own all copyrights not held by the publisher.

The information herein is offered for informational purposes solely and is universal as so. The presentation of the information is without a contract or any type of guarantee assurance.

The trademarks that are used are without any consent, and the publication of the trademark is without permission or backing by the trademark owner. All trademarks and brands within this book are for clarifying purposes only and are the owned by the owners themselves s, not affiliated with this document.

Table of Contents

Introduction

The image of the man, in charge of the barbecue, may be due to primitive times where the functions of men and women differed markedly. Women were in charge of gathering fruits and vegetables, sowing plants, taking care of the children and animals, maintaining cleanliness, etc., and men were in charge of hunting, with the objective of taking home the meat that would be grilled and would feed everyone in the tribe.

Although when we think of preparing grilled meals, we always imagine a man in this situation, who through this shows his masculinity by providing food for the household, this activity should not be attributed only to them, because women are as capable as men of preparing delicious meals, using a grill, especially when it is a grill with as many benefits as the Traeger Grill and Smoker.

Among the benefits of this model of grill are:

- Versatile, as it has the functionality to grill, smoke, bake, braise and roast, which will allow us to prepare various dishes, according to our preferences and needs.

- Convenience: It is easy to use and has automated controls that will do everything, or almost everything for you.

- Consistency: By maintaining a constant temperature that will give you the expected results.

- Community: Every day more and more people join the Traeger community, so you can share and discover ideas, tricks and tools, without forgetting the recipes.

All these benefits will make the experience of cooking on the grill an enriching and enjoyable one, where you can focus on spending time with family and friends and not on cooking on the grill.

And as we know that nothing compares to the flavor that smoke brings to food, it is necessary to emphasize that cooking food on the grill keeps its juices and all its nutritional properties, which will prevent the food from drying out and acquiring a lot of flavor, unlike cooking in other ways.

All these reasons will definitely enhance the experience of cooking with firewood and even more so when you try the delicious recipes you will find below.

Chapter 1: Traeger Grill

Appetizers, Sides & Snacks

1.   Traeger Grilled Spinach

(Ready in about: 20 minutes | Serving: 6 | Difficulty: Easy)

Nutrition per serving: Kcal 33 | Fat 1 g | Net Carbs 4 g | Protein 3 g

Ingredients

- 2 bunches of fresh spinach, washed and dried
- 1/2 teaspoon of salt
- 1 teaspoon of avocado oil

Instructions

1. Let the preheat to 400-425 °F.
2. Add salt, pepper, and avocado oil over spinach. Coat well.
3. Place spinach on the grill and cook for 4 to 5 minutes or until spinach is vibrant in color.
4. Serve hot.

2. Traeger Grilled Homemade Croutons

(Ready in about: 40 minutes | Serving: 8 | Difficulty: Easy)

Nutrition per serving: Kcal 188 | Fat 0 g | Net Carbs 20 g | Protein 4 g

Ingredients

- 2 tablespoons of Mediterranean blend seasoning
- 6 cups of cubed bread
- 1/4 cup of olive oil

Instructions

1. Let the grill preheat to 250 °F.
2. In a bowl, mix seasoning and oil and coat the bread cubes well.
3. On a baking sheet, place coated bread cubes.

4. Bake for 1/2 an hour or until golden brown, and stir every 5 minutes.

5. Serve warm.

3. Traeger Smoked Mac & Cheese

(Ready in about: 1 hour and 5 minutes | Serving: 8 | Difficulty: Easy)

Nutrition per serving: Kcal 528 | Fat 40 g | Net Carbs 26 g | Protein 5g

Ingredients

- 2 and 1/2 cups of small pasta shells, cooked

- 1/3 cup of flour

- 6 cups of whole milk

- 1/2 teaspoon of salt

- 2 cups of cheddar jack cheese

- 1/2 teaspoon of dry mustard

- 1/2 cup of salted butter

- A dash of Worcestershire sauce

- 2 cups of smoked white cheddar

- 1 cup of crushed Ritz

Instructions

1. Let the grill preheat for 5-10 minutes; on "Smoke," keep the lid open until a fire is established. Turn the grill to 325 °F and now close the lid.

2. Melt butter on medium flame, add in flour. Keep whisking and cook for 5 to 6 minutes until color changes to light tan.

3. Add in Worcestershire sauce, milk, dry mustard, and salt. Mix until the sauce thickens.

4. Add in the pasta shells and 1 cup of cheese mix well.

5. Put this mix in a 10 by 13 oiled baking dish and top with cheese and the crushed Ritz.

6. Let the Traeger preheat to 325 °F. Bake for 1/2 an hour or until cheese is melted and bubbly. Serve right away.

4. Roasted Elk Jalapeno Poppers

(Ready in about: 45 minutes | Serving: 10 | Difficulty: Easy)

Nutrition per serving: Kcal 153 | Fat 8.9 g | Net Carbs 7.9 g | Protein 12 g

Ingredients

- 1 and 1/2 cups of garlic & herb-flavored cream cheese
- 1 cup of Worcestershire sauce
- 1 cup of lime juice
- 10 pieces of bacon
- 1 cup of light soy sauce
- 4 steaks of elk
- 20 jalapeno peppers
- Honey, to taste

Instructions

1. In a bowl, mix soy sauce, lime juice, and Worcestershire sauce. Add sliced steaks to cover it, and keep in the fridge for 4-6 hours or overnight.

2. Let the grill preheat to 350 °F, keep the lid closed.

3. Cut the jalapenos lengthwise, take out the seeds.

4. Slice the bacon in half.

5. Add cream cheese into jalapenos halves.

6. Attach 1 slice of elk with jalapeno, wrap with 1 piece of bacon. Secure with toothpick

7. Grill at 350 °F, for 10-15 minutes, until jalapenos are charred and soft.

8. Take off from grill and top with honey and serve.

Chapter 2: Traeger Grill Pork Recipes

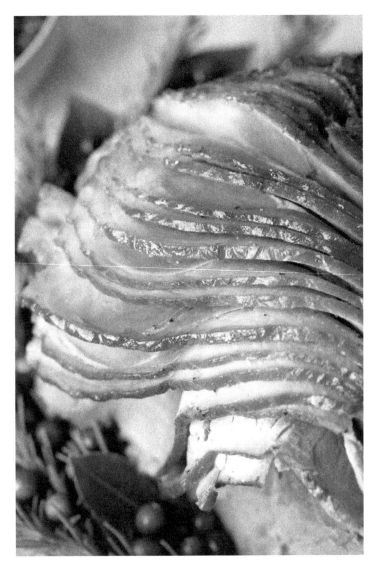

5. Smoked Spiral Ham with Honey Glaze

(Ready in about: 3 hours and 20 minutes | Serving: 12| Difficulty: Medium)

Nutrition per serving: Kcal 321| Fat 19 g| Net Carbs 13 g| Protein 21 g

Ingredients

- 8-10 pounds of smoked spiral ham

Honey Glaze:

- 1 cup of packed brown sugar

- 3 tablespoons of honey

- 2 and 1/4 cups of ginger ale

- 1 and 1/2 teaspoons of Dijon mustard

- 4 and 1/2 teaspoons of apple cider vinegar

- 2 cloves of minced garlic

Instructions

1. In a pan, mix brown sugar, apple cider vinegar, ginger ale, and honey. Let it boil and reduce it by half, cook for almost 15 minutes. Add in the rest of the ingredients. Except for pork. Cook for 5 minutes. Turn off the heat.

2. Clean and trim the ham, pour honey glaze between the pieces. Do not completely detach the pieces and brush with the remaining glaze.

3. Let the Traeger smoker preheat to 230-240 °F.

4. Place the glazed ham in a tray and put the tray in Traeger, and close the lid. Keep basting the ham after every 20 minutes.

5. It will take 3 hours. Serve right away

6. Easy Smoked Pork Butt

(Ready in about: 17 hours and 15 minutes | Serving:

16| Difficulty: Medium)

Nutrition per serving: Kcal 217| Fat 10 g| Net Carbs

4g| Protein 27 g

Ingredients

- 8-10 pounds of pork shoulder, bone-in roast

- 3 tablespoons of yellow mustard

- 1/2 cup of sweet & smoky rub

Instructions

1. Let the Traeger grill preheat to 225 °F.

2. Safe 1 tablespoon of sweet & smoky rub for later use.

3. Cover the cleaned pork shoulder with yellow mustard. Cover in sweet & smoky rub; make sure it is covered well.

4. Place the coated pork on grill grates. Close the lid.

5. Smoke until internal temperature reaches 195 °F or 201 °F. Total time will be 15-20 hours.

6. Let it rest for 1 hour. Sprinkle the reserved rub all over and serve.

7. Cider Brined Pulled Pork

(Ready in about: 9 hours and 15 minutes | Serving: 24 | Difficulty: Medium)

Nutrition per serving: Kcal 243 | Fat 8 g | Net Carbs 14g | Protein 23 g

Ingredients

- 8 pounds of pork butt
- 8 cups of apple cider

Rub Ingredients:

- 5 tablespoons of brown sugar
- 2 tablespoons of smoked paprika
- 1 tablespoon of garlic powder
- 2 tablespoons of kosher salt
- 5 tablespoons of sugar
- 1 tablespoon of black pepper
- 1 tablespoon of onion powder

Instructions

1. In a bowl, add all the rub ingredients. Mix until sugar and salt are dissolved.

2. In a large pot, add apple cider. Add in 1/2 of the rub ingredients. Mix well. Add in the pork butt keep it submerged.

3. Keep in the fridge for 8 hours and less than 12 hours — It is important.

4. Keep safe the rest of the rub ingredients.

5. Let the smoker preheat to 225 °F. Keep the lid closed. Keep safe the brine and pat dry the pork. With the reserved rub, massage the pork.

6. Place meat on grill grates directly, keep the fatty side up — Cook for 3 hours. After every hour, brush the pork with marinade.

7. Add 4-6 cups of brine to a pot and let it boil.

8. Raise the temperature of the smoker to 250 °F after 3 hours.

9. Place the roast in aluminum foil, add 2 cups of boiled brine in, and cook for 6-8 hours or until the thickest part's internal temperature reaches 200 °F.

10. Cover the meat with aluminum foil if it is browning too much.

11. Let it rest for 20 minutes. Slice and serve.

8. Easy Smoked Pork Loin

(Ready in about: 3 hours and 20 minutes | Serving: 24 | Difficulty: Medium)

Nutrition per serving: Kcal 231 | Fat 7 g | Net Carbs 11 g | Protein 28 g

Ingredients

- Pork Loin Dry rub, as needed

- 10-11 pounds of pork loin

Instructions

1. Let the grill preheat to 220 °F. May use combination pellets for this recipe.

2. Clean and trim the pork loin.

3. Rub the dry rub on pork. Let it rest at room temperature for 30 minutes.

4. Place meat directly on grill grates fat side up, cook for 2-3 hours at 220 °F until internal temperature reaches 145 °F.

5. Let it rest for 10 minutes. Slice and serve.

9. Smoked Pork Chops with Ale-Balsamic Glaze

(Ready in about: 1 hour and 20 minutes | Serving: 4 | Difficulty: Medium)

Nutrition per serving: Kcal 211 | Fat 8 g | Net Carbs 10.7 g | Protein 23.7 g

Ingredients

- 4 8-ounce chops bone-in pork
- 1/2 cup of balsamic vinegar
- 3/4 cup of ginger ale
- 1/4 cup of brown sugar
- Traeger Pork & Poultry rub
- 2 sprigs of rosemary, chopped

Instructions

1. Let the Traeger preheat to 165 °F, keep the lid closed for 15 minutes, and use super smoke if possible.

2. Coat the pork well in Pork & Poultry rub.

3. Place the ribs on grill grates and smoke for 1/2 an hour.

4. Additionally, add balsamic vinegar, ginger ale, rosemary leaves, and brown sugar in a pan on medium flame until it becomes a slightly thick cook for 15-20 minutes.

5. Take out the ribs, let the smoker's temperature rise to 500 °F, and preheat with the lid closed for 15 minutes.

6. Drizzle olive oil on ribs and cook for 5 minutes at 500 °F.

7. Flip the ribs and baste with glaze. Cook until the internal temperature reaches 145 °F or until 5 minutes.

8. Let it rest 10 minutes before slicing.

10. Traeger Smoked Stuffed Pork Tenderloin

(Ready in about: 80 minutes | Serving: 8 | Difficulty: Medium)

Nutrition per serving: Kcal 610 | Fat 31 g | Net Carbs 5 g | Protein 23 g

Ingredients

- 1/2 cup of cheddar cheese

- 1 cup of spinach leaves

- 1 pork tenderloin

- 1 pound of sliced bacon

- 1/2 cup of provolone cheese

Rub:

- 1/2 teaspoon of granulated garlic

- 1 teaspoon of red pepper flake

- 1 teaspoon of salt

- 1 teaspoon of paprika

- 1/2 teaspoon of onion powder

- 1/4 teaspoon of cumin

- 1/2 teaspoon of pepper

Instructions

1. Let the grill preheat to 325 °F.

2. In the center of the tenderloin, place spinach leaves on the whole length of the tenderloin.

3. Place cheese on top of tenderloin.

4. Roll the tenderloin, so the cheese and spinach are inside.

5. In a bowl, add all the ingredients of rub, coat the tenderloin in this rub mix.

6. Wrap the tenderloin in bacon.

7. Put wrapped tenderloin in the middle of the rack and cook for 1 hour until internal temperature reaches 145 °F

8. Take out from grill rest and slice.

11. Perfect Cheeseburger

(Ready in about: 40 minutes | Serving: 4 | Difficulty: Easy)

Nutrition per serving: Kcal 198 | Fat 9 g | Net Carbs 11 g | Protein 13.5 g

Ingredients

- Sliced vegetables, to your liking (tomatoes slices, onion rings, lettuce leaves)

- 4 hamburger patties

- Condiments, to taste (ketchup, mayonnaise)

Instructions

1. For this recipe, use hickory pellets. Let the smoker preheat to 425-450 °F with the lid closed.

2. Place patties on the grill and cook for 8 to 9 minutes with a closed lid.

3. Flip patties cook for another 9 minutes until the internal thermometer reaches 160 °F.

4. Add cheese and melt it.

5. Serve with your favorite sliced vegetables and condiments.

Chapter 3: Traeger Grill Beef

Recipes

12. Smoked Tri-Tip

(Ready in about: 2 hours and 15 minutes | Serving: 8 |

Difficulty: Medium)

Nutrition per serving: Kcal 244 | Fat 13 g | Net Carb 0

g | Protein 29 g

Ingredients

- Roasted garlic blend

- 1 beef roast tri-tip

Instructions

1. Preheat the Traeger to 175 °F.

2. Coat the beef with seasoning, generously.

3. Place on grill and cook for 90 minutes.

4. Transfer to a plate cover with foil.

5. Preheat the Traeger to 400-450 °F.

6. Place the steak on the grill and cook until the

   doneness you want.

7. Rest it before serving.

13. Brisket Chili

(Ready in about: 60 minutes | Serving: 12 | Difficulty: Medium)

Nutrition per serving: Kcal 385 | Fat 8 g | Net Carbs 17 g | Protein 31 g

Ingredients

- 15 ounces of tomato sauce

- 4 cups of cooked brisket, diced

- 1 can of chili beans

- 2 cans of stewed tomatoes

- 8 cups of water

- Sour cream, to your taste

- 1 package of chili kit

- 1 can drain of pinto beans

- Cheese, as needed

Instructions

1. In a pot, add all ingredients except for beans.

2. Let it simmer on low heat for 45 minutes. Add in beans.

3. Preheat the Traeger to 375 °F.

4. Place the pot on the grill and cook for 1/2 an hour.

5. Serve with cheese and sour cream.

14. Traeger Smoked Mississippi Pot Roast

(Ready in about: 5 hours and 15 minutes | Serving: 8| Difficulty: Medium)

Nutrition per serving: Kcal 314| Fat 13 g| Net Carbs 4 g| Protein 39 g

Ingredients

- 1 stick of salted butter

- 5 pounds of beef roast chuck

- 1 teaspoon of black pepper

- 1 teaspoon of paprika

- 1 teaspoon of onion powder

- 8 pepperoncini peppers

- 1/4 cup of carrots, chopped

- 1 packet of au jus mix

- 1 teaspoon of salt

- 1/2 teaspoon of granulated garlic

- 1 packet of dressing dry ranch mix

- 1/2 a cup of water

Instructions

1. Coat the roast with all dry spices.

2. Sear the roast in cast iron on each side.

3. Preheat the Traeger grill to 275 °F.

4. In a large grill-safe pan, add seared meat with butter, ranch mix, pepperoncini, water, carrots, jus, and garlic. Place this pan on the grill and close the lid.

5. Let it cook and monitor so it would not burn after every hour.

6. Cook until it becomes fork tender or internal temperature reaches 200-205 °F.

7. Serve with bread and mashed potatoes.

15. Philly Cheese Steak Sandwich

(Ready in about: 25 minutes | Serving: 4 | Difficulty: Medium)

Nutrition per serving: Kcal 673 | Fat 47 g | Net Carbs 37 g | Protein 47 g

Ingredients

- 4 buns
- 1.5 pounds of thinly sliced rib-eye steak
- 1 thinly sliced onion
- 1 tablespoon of canola oil
- 1 thinly sliced bell pepper
- 4 slices of cheese
- 1/2 teaspoon of Pepper
- 1 teaspoon of salt

Instructions

1. Preheat the Traeger to 450 °F.

2. Put a cast-iron pan on the grill and heat for 15 minutes. Add oil, green peppers, onion. Cook until translucent.

3. Add in seasoned steak with pepper and salt — Cook for 4 to 5 minutes.

4. Place in buns with cheese slices grill the whole sandwich for 3-4 minutes.

16. Mini Smoked Meatloaf

(Ready in about: 1 hour | Serving: 4| Difficulty: Medium)

Nutrition per serving: Kcal 799| Fat 46 g| Net Carbs 53 g| Protein 41 g

Ingredients

Meatloaf:

- 1 pound of ground beef
- 1 egg
- 1/2 cup of chopped onion
- 1 cup of shredded cheddar cheese
- 3/4 cup of milk
- 1/2 cup of quick-cooking oats
- 1 teaspoon of salt

Toppings:

- 1 teaspoon of mustard
- 1/2 cup of ketchup
- 1/3 cup of brown sugar packed

Instructions

1. Preheat the Traeger to 350 °F.

2. In a bowl, whisk milk and egg. Add in salt, oats, cheese, and onion. Mix well and add in the beef. Make into 8   mini loaves.

3. In a bowl, mix topping ingredients

4. Place loaves on the grill. Pour topping sauce over.

5. Cook for 45 minutes, with the lid, closed until no longer pink.

6. Serve hot

17. Grilled New York Strip

(Ready in about: 20 minutes | Serving: 6| Difficulty:

Medium)

Nutrition per serving: Kcal 198| Fat 14 g| Net Carbs

0 g| Protein 17 g

Ingredients

- Salt and pepper, to taste

- 3 New York strips

Instructions

1. Keep the steak at room temperature for 1/2 an

   hour before cooking.

2. Preheat the Traeger to 450 °F.

3. Coat the meat with salt and pepper and place on

   the grill.

4. Cook each side for 5 to 7 minutes

5. Cook until the internal temperature reaches 125-128 °F.

6. Rest the meat and serve.

Smoked Beef Ribs

(Ready in about: 5 hours and 15 minutes | Serving: 6| Difficulty: Medium)

Nutrition per serving: Kcal 954| Fat 65 g| Net Carbs 35 g| Protein 53 g

Ingredients

- 3 cups of Barbecue sauce

- 5 pounds of beef ribs

- 3 tablespoons of Beef rub

Instructions

1. Season the ribs with a dry rub, and Preheat the Traeger to 180 °F, or Smoke mode.

2. Put seasoned meat on grill and cook for 2 hours.

3. Raise the temperature of the grill to 275 °F, cook the meat for 2 hours more.

4. Raise the temperature of the grill to 325 °F, now baste with BBQ sauce every 10-15 minutes, in the last hour, until meat is fork-tender.

5. Let it rest for 10   minutes, then serve.

Chapter 4: Traeger Grill

Poultry Recipes

18. Citrus Turkey

(Ready in about: 4 hours | Serving: 12| Difficulty:
Medium)

Nutrition per serving: Kcal 351 | Fat 13 g | Net Carbs
9 g | Protein 37 g

Ingredients

- 1 15–pound Turkey

- 3 oranges

- 1 tablespoon of garlic powder

- 3 lemons

- 1 tablespoon of onion powder

- 3 tablespoons of salt

- 2 tablespoons of Italian seasoning

- 3 limes

- Italian seasoning, as needed

- Poultry seasoning, as needed

- Minced Fresh herbs: One teaspoon

Instructions

1. In a bowl, add Italian seasoning, garlic, onion powder, and salt. Mix well. Coat the bird well in a dry rub for 1-3 days.

2. On the grill, layer limes, herbs, oranges, and lemon in a pan. Place the bird on top.

3. Season the bird with spices and butter.

4. Preheat the Traeger to 275 °F with the lid closed for 15 Minutes.

5. Cook for 3 and a half hours until the internal temperature of the bird reaches 165 F.

6. Serve hot.

19. Herb Buttered Chicken

(Ready in about: 3 hours | Serving: 12| Difficulty: Medium)

Nutrition per serving: Kcal 323|Fat 15 g| Net Carbs 8 g| Protein 32 g

Ingredients

- 1 butter stick

- 2 teaspoons of chipotle chili powder

- Basil, 1 teaspoon

- 2 teaspoons of garlic powder

- Thyme, 1 teaspoon

Instructions

1. Cut the chicken open, lay it flat.

2. Melt 1 stick of butter mix well with chipotle chili and garlic powder.

3. Fill up the seasoning injection and inject into chicken breast till it swells, then in legs and thighs.

4. Sprinkle with basil and thyme.

5. Preheat the Traeger to 275 °F with the lid closed for 15 minutes. Place chicken on grill and smoke for 45 with the lid closed.

6. After 45 minutes, raise the temperature to 350 °F, cook for 1 hour or until the internal temperature reaches 165 °F

7. Before slicing the chicken, let it rest and serve.

20. Smoked Hassel back Pesto Chicken

(Ready in about: 3 hours | Serving: 12| Difficulty: Medium)

Nutrition per serving: Kcal 345 | Fat 17 g | Net Carbs 9 g | Protein 39 g

Ingredients

- Pesto sauce, enough to coat chicken breasts

- 2 Chicken breasts

- Mozzarella, to taste

- Italian seasoning, enough to coat chicken breasts

Instructions

1. Rub chicken with Italian seasoning and score the chicken.

2. Preheat the Traeger to 350 °F with the lid closed for 15 minutes.

3. Place chicken directly on grill cook until internal temperature reaches 150 °F.

4. Put on mozzarella cheese on top, cook until melted.

5. Serve hot.

21. Smoked Herb Butter Turkey

(Ready in about: 4 hours | Serving: 12| Difficulty: Medium)

Nutrition per serving: Kcal 437 | Fat 21.3 g | Net Carbs 11 g | Protein 37 g

Ingredients

- 2 Butter sticks

- Different fresh herbs mixture

- Italian seasoning

- Chicken seasoning

- 1 Whole turkey

Instructions

1. In a bowl, mix fresh chopped herbs with room temperature butter, mix well, spread parchment paper, and roll into a log. Keep in the freezer.

2. Preheat the Traeger to 200 °F with the lid closed for 15 minutes.

3. Put the turkey on a grill with herb butter under the turkey's skin.

4. Smoke for 1/2 an hour at 200 °F.

5. Cook at 325 **F** for 2 to 3 hours until the meat's internal temperature reaches 165 °**F**.

6. Rest and serve.

22. Grilled Chicken Salad

(Ready in about: 2 hours and 20 minutes | Serving: 12| Difficulty: Easy)

Nutrition per serving: Kcal 367| Fat 19.3 g| Net Carbs 21 g| Protein 36 g

Ingredients

- 1/2 cup of plain yogurt

- 4 green onions

- 1 whole chicken

- 1/2 cup of mayonnaise

- 1 lemon

- Cumin

- 1 tablespoon brown sugar

- 4 stalks of celery

- 1 cup of red grapes

- Fresh dill

- 1 cup of green grapes

Instructions

1. Break the chicken down into breasts, thighs, legs, and wings

2. Rub the chicken with poultry seasoning.

3. Smoke at 250 °F until internal temperature reaches 165 °F.

4. Take all bones out of cooked chicken and shred.

5. Chop celery, green onions into bite-size pieces

6. Cut grapes in half.

7. In a large bowl, add all chopped up ingredients.

8. In another bowl, add 1/2 cup mayo, 1/2 cup yogurt, lemon juice, dill, sugar, salt, cumin, and pepper. Mix well

9. Pour dressing over chopped ingredients, mix well and serve.

23. Honey Balsamic Chicken Legs

(Ready in about: 5 hours and 20 minutes | Serving: 12 | Difficulty: Medium)

Nutrition per serving: Kcal 367 | Fat 19.3 g | Net Carbs 21 g | Protein 36 g

Ingredients

- 10-12 chicken legs
- 2 teaspoons of minced garlic
- 1 cup of honey
- 1 cup of balsamic vinegar
- 1/2 cup of dark brown sugar
- 1 cup of pineapple juice
- 1 cup of soy sauce
- 1 teaspoon of Sriracha

Instructions

1. In a bowl, add all ingredients, mix well.

2. Coat chicken legs in marinade and place in a large zip lock bag with marinade.

3. Keep in the fridge for 4 hours or overnight.

4. Preheat the Traeger to 325 °F, and place the chicken directly on grates. Do not discard marinade.

5. Let the chicken cook and add marinade into a saucepot. Simmer for 20-30 minutes and reduce by half.

6. Cook chicken for 35-45 minutes; raise the temperature to 450 °F for the last 15 minutes.

7. Serve with sauce.

24. Mayo & Herb Roasted Turkey

(Ready in about: 4 hours and 20 minutes | Serving: 8 | Difficulty: Medium)

Nutrition per serving: Kcal 342 | Fat 13 g | Net Carbs 13 g | Protein 35 g

Ingredients

- 1 12-pound turkey
- 1 and 1/4 cup of mayonnaise
- 1/4 teaspoon of honey
- Salt and pepper, to taste
- 1/3 cup of fresh herbs, chopped

Instructions

1. Preheat the Traeger to 425 °F with the lid closed for 15 minutes
2. In a bowl, mix herbs and mayo. Add ¼ teaspoon of honey mix well.
3. Clean the turkey and pat dry.

4. Coat the turkey with mayo mix—season with pepper and salt.

5. Add fresh rosemary, thyme in the bird cavity, tie the legs together.

6. Roast turkey for 1/2 an hour-45 minutes.

7. As turkey is cooking, lower temperature to 350 °F.

8. Cook until the internal temperature reaches.

9. Roast until internal temperature reaches 160 °F in the breast part and 175 °F in the thigh.

10. Rest before slicing.

Chapter 5: Traeger Grill

Seafood Recipes

25. Salmon Miso Poke Bowl

(Ready in about: 2 hours and 15 minutes | Serving: 4 | Difficulty: Easy)

Nutrition per serving: Kcal 481 | Fat 30 g | Net Carbs 33 g | Protein 23 g

Ingredients

For Salmon:

- 1/2 teaspoon sesame oil
- 2 cups of fresh salmon, cut into cubes
- 1 tablespoon of red miso
- 3 tablespoons of soy sauce
- 1/2 teaspoon of ginger, minced
- 3 tablespoons of green onions, white parts only
- 1 tablespoon of rice wine vinegar
- Sushi rice
- 1/2 teaspoon of minced garlic

Toppings:

- Sliced avocados

- Shelled edamame

- Sriracha

- Nori slices

- Diced green onions

- Diced cucumbers

- Sesame seeds

Instructions

1. In a bowl, add all marinade ingredients with salmon and keep in the fridge for 1-2 hours.

2. Add a spoonful of salmon poke on sushi rice and serve with the desired topping.

26. Salmon Orzo Pasta Salad

(Ready in about: 50 minutes | Serving: 8 | Difficulty: Easy)

Nutrition per serving: Kcal 365 | Fat 11 g | Net Carbs 45 g | Protein 20 g

Ingredients

- 1 grilled salmon fillet

- 2 cups of orzo, uncooked

- 1 handful of baby spinach

- 1/4 cup of diced red bell peppers

- 1 cup of crumbled feta

- 1 cup sliced in half, cherry tomatoes

- 1 cucumber, diced

- 1 cup of Greek freak dressing

- 1/4 cup of Kalamata olives

Instructions

1. Cook pasta in well-salted water. Rinse with cold water,

2. In a large bowl, mix the pasta with baby spinach, bell peppers, cherry tomatoes, feta, olives, and cucumber.

3. Pour over dressing mix gently add grilled salmon mix lightly and serve.

27. Grilled Salmon Sandwich

(Ready in about: 60 minutes | Serving: 4 | Difficulty: Medium)

Nutrition per serving: Kcal 652 | Fat 33 g | Net Carbs 25 g | Protein 50 g

Ingredients

Salmon Sandwiches:

- Fin & Feather Traeger rub
- 4 salmon sandwich-sized filets
- 1 teaspoon of salt
- 1 tablespoon of olive oil
- Lettuce
- 4 toasted buns

Dill Aioli:

- 1/4 teaspoon of salt
- 1/2 cup of mayonnaise
- 1/2 teaspoon of minced fresh dill

- 2 teaspoons of lemon juice

- 1/2 teaspoon of lemon zest

Instructions

1. In a bowl, add all ingredients of dill mayo, mix well and keep in the fridge.

2. Preheat the Traeger to 425-450 °F

3. coat fish filet with olive oil, salt, and then seasoning rub.

4. Place fish on grill cook until the internal temperature of fish reaches 130-135 °F

5. Let it rest for 5 minutes before placing it in a bun.

6. Top with aioli, lettuce, and serve.

28. Traeger Grilled Shrimp Scampi

(Ready in about: 15 minutes | Serving: 4| Difficulty: Medium)

Nutrition per serving: Kcal 298| Fat 24 g| Net Carbs 2 g| Protein 16 g

Ingredients

- 1 pound of the colossal tail-on raw shrimp
- 1/2 teaspoon of chopped fresh garlic
- 1/2 cup of melted salted butter
- 1/2 teaspoon of garlic powder
- 1/4 cup of dry white wine
- 1/2 teaspoon of salt
- 1 tablespoon of lemon juice

Instructions

1. Preheat the Traeger to 400 °F with the cast iron skillet.

2. In a bowl, mix garlic, melted butter, lemon juice, and white wine.

3. Pour in the cast iron pan, let it heat for 3-4 minutes.

4. Coat the shrimp with salt and garlic powder — place in cast iron skillet.

5. Grill for 10   minutes with lid closed; make sure not to overcook shrimp.

6. Serve right away.

29. Red Snapper Recipe

(Ready in about: 2 hours | Serving: 4| Difficulty: Medium)

Nutrition per serving: Kcal 281| Fat 13 g| Net Carbs 4 g| Protein 25 g

Ingredients

- 1 lime
- 1 teaspoon of black pepper
- 4 large red snapper filets
- 1/3 cup of olive oil
- 2 onions
- 1 teaspoon of minced garlic
- 1 teaspoon of salt
- 1/2 teaspoon of cumin
- 3 teaspoons of fresh cilantro
- 1/4 cup of Ponzu sauce

- 1 teaspoon of ancho chili powder

- 1/2 teaspoon of lime zest

Instructions

1. Cut the lime into slices. Cut onions into rings and break them apart.

2. In the olive oil, whisk all ingredients.

3. Preheat the Traeger to 350 °F.

4. On top of lime and onion slice, place the fish and coat with olive oil mix.

5. After every 15 minutes, baste the fish. Cook until flaky and firm.

6. Serve right away.

30. Traeger Grilled Crab Legs

(Ready in about: 55 minutes | Serving: 6| Difficulty: Medium)

Nutrition per serving: Kcal 765| Fat 38 g| Net Carbs 1 g| Protein 99 g

Ingredients

- 1 cup of melted butter

- 4-6 pounds of snow crab leg

- 2 cloves of minced garlic

- 3 tablespoons of chopped fresh parsley

- 2-3 tablespoons of Old Bay seasoning

- 1/4 cup of dry white wine

Instructions

1. Preheat the Traeger to 375 °F.

2. Put Crab in foil pan. Mix all other ingredients and pour over crab.

3. Place on grill cook with closed lid.

4. Cook for 10   minutes, baste with juices, cook for another 10 minutes.

5. Baste again and cook for 5-10 minutes.

6. Serve right away.

31. BBQ Salmon with Bourbon Glaze

(Ready in about: 2 hours | Serving: 4 | Difficulty: Medium)

Nutrition per serving: Kcal 281 | Fat 18 g | Net Carbs 2 g | Protein 22 g

Ingredients

- 1 tablespoon of olive oil
- 1 cup of ketchup
- 1 cup of Jim beam bourbon
- 1/4 cup of apple cider vinegar
- 3 teaspoons of Worcestershire sauce
- 1/2 cup of brown sugar
- 1 tablespoon of lemon juice
- 1 tablespoon of yellow mustard
- 1/2 teaspoon of minced garlic
- 1/2 teaspoon of black pepper
- 1 teaspoon of salt

- 2 tablespoon of dry rub seasoning

Instructions

1. Preheat the Traeger to 350 °F.

2. Coat dry fish with olive oil and rub with seasoning.

3. In a bowl, add the rest of the ingredients and mix well.

4. Put salmon on the grill, cook for 5 minutes, brush with glaze generously, and cook for 10 minutes.

5. Again, brush with glaze, flip the fish and glaze the other side.

6. Cook until the internal temperature reaches 145 °F.

7. Serve right away.

Chapter 6: Traeger Grill Lamb

Recipes

32. Lamb Burgers with Pickled Onions

(Ready in about: 60 minutes | Serving: 4 | Difficulty: Medium)

Nutrition per serving: Kcal 236 | Fat 14 g | Net Carbs 13 g | Protein 17 g

Ingredients

- 1 pound of ground lamb
- Red onion, 1/2 cut into slices and 1/2 diced
- 1/2 teaspoon of kosher salt
- 1 cup of Greek yogurt
- 2 tablespoons of lemon juice
- 6 tablespoons of lime juice
- 5 cloves of minced garlic
- 2 tablespoons of chopped herbs like mint, parsley, and dill
- 1 tablespoon of olive oil
- 1/2 teaspoon of raw cane sugar

- 1 and 1/2 teaspoons of ground cumin

- 2 tablespoons of minced fresh dill

- 1 cup of ground pork

- 3 tablespoons of minced parsley

- Cucumber, cut into pieces

- 1 teaspoon of ground coriander

- 3 tablespoons of minced fresh mint

- Black pepper

- 6   buns

- Tomato slices

- Butter lettuce

Instructions

1. In a bowl, add lime juice, 1/2 teaspoon of sugar, 1/2 teaspoon of salt, thinly sliced onion. Mix well and let it sit for 2 hours in the fridge.

2. In another bowl, add yogurt, ¼ teaspoon of minced garlic, lemon juice, mixed chopped

herbs, 1/2 teaspoon of salt, mix well and cover it, keep in the fridge.

3. In a pan, in warm olive oil, sauté onion for 7 minutes.

4. In a bowl, mix coriander, pork, parsley, cooled sautéed onion, mint, lamb, salt, pepper, garlic, dill, cumin. Mix well but do not over mix.

5. Make 6 meat patties. Cook right away or keep in the fridge for 8 hours.

6. Preheat the grill to high.

7. Put burgers on the grill and cook for 2-3 minutes on each side until cooked well.

8. Rest the burgers for 5 minutes off the grill.

9. Serve burgers in buns with yogurt sauce, pickled onion slices of vegetables.

33. Slow Roasted BBQ Lamb Shoulder

(Ready in about: 5 hours | Serving: 4 | Difficulty: Medium)

Nutrition per serving: Kcal 312 | Fat 15 g | Net Carbs 9 g | Protein 25 g

Ingredients

- 1/4 teaspoon of cumin seeds

- 1 tablespoon of smoked paprika

- 1 tablespoon of lemon juice

- 1/4 teaspoon of coriander seeds

- 3 cloves of garlic

- 1 tablespoon of mint, chopped

- 2 tablespoons + 1/2 cup of water:

- 4 tablespoons of olive oil

- 1/4 teaspoon of caraway seeds

- 1 tablespoon of salt

- 3 pound of lamb shoulders

- 1 and 1/2 cups of Greek yogurt

- 2 ounce of ancho chilies, dried, remove seeds

- 1 tablespoon of fresh chopped dill

- 1/4 cup cucumber, grated

- Juice and zest of 1 lemon

- Salt and pepper, to taste

Instructions

1. In a grinder, add all seeds finely grind them.

2. In a bowl, add ancho chilies and 2 tablespoons of water and microwave for 2 minutes on high.

3. Add this chili mix to a blender and add lemon juice, 2 tablespoons of oil, 2 garlic cloves, ground spices, 1 tablespoon of salt, paprika. Pulse on high until pureed.

4. In a pan, place Lamb and rub 1/2 of the pureed sauce all over. Let it rest at room temperature for 2 hours.

5. Preheat the Traeger to 325 °F; keep the lid closed for 15 minutes.

6. Pour 1/2 cup of water into pan cover with foil — Cook for 2 and a half hours.

7. Keep adding water in the pan if required.

8. Uncover and let it cook for 2 and a half hours, till lamb is tender and brown. Baste often with juice at the bottom of the pan.

9. Let it rest for 20 minutes off the grill.

10. In a bowl, add the rest of the ingredients, mix well.

11. Serve the shredded pork with yogurt sauce.

34. Braised Irish Lamb Stew

(Ready in about: 3 hours | Serving: 4 | Difficulty: Medium)

Nutrition per serving: Kcal 352 | Fat 13 g | Net Carbs 14 g | Protein 26 g

Ingredients

- 4 pound of boneless lamb shoulder, cut into 1" pieces
- 2 tablespoons of olive oil
- 1 diced onion
- 1/2 cup of white wine
- 1 cup of chopped bacon
- 4 cup of beef stock
- 2 cloves of minced garlic
- 2 carrots, cut into cubes
- 2 sprigs of fresh thyme
- 1 sprig of fresh rosemary

- 2 bay leaves

- 1/4 cup of flour

- 2 potatoes, cut into cubes

- Salt and pepper, to taste

- 1/4 cup of butter, at room temperature

Instructions

1. Preheat the Traeger to 350 °F, keep the lid closed for 15 minutes.

2. Sprinkle salt and pepper to season the lamb. In a Dutch oven, add 2 tablespoons of olive oil, brown the lamb on all sides set it aside.

3. Cook bacon for 15-20 minutes, until crispy and browned. Keep safe 2 tablespoons of bacon fat.

4. Sauté onion in bacon fat until translucent. Add garlic cook for 30 seconds.

5. Add lamb back to Dutch oven, add white wine, and deglaze.

6. Add carrots, stock, potatoes, and herbs, let it simmer.

7. Cover it and place it on the grill at 350 °F.

8. Let it for 1 and a half to 2 hours, until Lamb is falling-apart tender.

9. Take out from the grill and place back on the stovetop. Mix flour and butter, and pour into the stew — Cook for 5-10 minutes. Add pepper and salt.

10. Take out bay leaves and sprigs and serve.

Chapter 7: Traeger Grill

Vegetables Recipes

35. Smoked Hummus with Roasted Vegetables

(Ready in about: 55minutes| Serving: 4| Difficulty: Medium)

Nutrition per serving: Kcal 192 | Fat 9 g| Net Carb 9 g| Protein 20 g

Ingredients

- 1 and 1/2 cups of chickpeas

- 1/3 cup of tahini

- 6 tablespoons of olive oil

- 1 thinly sliced onion

- 1 tablespoon of garlic minced

- 1 teaspoon of salt

- 2 cups of cauliflower florets

- 4 tablespoons of lemon juice

- 2 cups of fresh Brussels sprouts

- 2 cups of butternut squash

- 2 Portobello mushrooms

- Salt and black pepper

Instructions

1. Preheat the Traeger to 180 °F.

2. On a baking sheet, add chickpeas and smoke for 15-20 minutes.

3. In a bowl, add all other ingredients (except for vegetables) with chickpeas. Pulse until combined.

4. Preheat the grill to high.

5. Coat vegetables with oil and roast for 15-20 minutes on a baking sheet.

6. Serve roasted vegetables with smoked hummus.

36. Baked Creamed Spinach

(Ready in about: 45 minutes | Serving: 6 | Difficulty: Easy)

Nutrition per serving: Kcal 187 | Fat 8 g | Net Carb 3 g | Protein 12 g

Ingredients

- 1 chopped shallot

- 1 and 1/2 cups of heavy cream

- 2 10-ounce packages of frozen spinach, thawed

- 1 teaspoon of red pepper flakes

- 2 tablespoons of butter

- 2 cloves of garlic

- 3/4 cup of sour cream

- 1 teaspoon of ground nutmeg

- Salt and black pepper, to taste

- 1/2 cup of parmesan cheese, panko breadcrumbs, and Romano cheese, each

Instructions

1. In a pan, sauté garlic, shallot in butter. Cook for 3 minutes, add chili flakes and cook for two more minutes.

2. Add nutmeg and cream let it boil. Add black pepper and salt.

3. Add sour cream, spinach, add more seasoning if required.

4. Take off from heat and add in cheese.

5. Remove from heat and stir in cheeses.

6. Transfer to a baking dish and sprinkle panko on top.

7. Pour mixture into a baking dish and top with panko.

8. Cook in Traeger at 375 °F, for 1/2 an hour, with the lid closed.

37. Butter Braised Green Beans

(Ready in about: 1 hour and 15 minutes | Serving: 6 |

Difficulty: Easy)

Nutrition per serving: Kcal 131 | Fat 9 g | Net Carb 6

g | Protein 30 g

Ingredients

- Traeger Veggie rub

- 24 ounces of trimmed green beans

- 8 tablespoons of butter, melted

Instructions

1. Preheat the Traeger to 325 °F.

2. On a baking sheet, add beans, coat with melted

   butter

3. Season with the veggie rub.

4. Roast for 60 minutes, keep stirring every 20

   minutes, until light brown in places.

38. Traeger Stuffed Peppers

(Ready in about: 21 minutes| Serving: 6| Difficulty:

Medium)

Nutrition per serving: Kcal 422 | Fat 22 g| Net Carb

24 g| Protein 34 g

Ingredients

- 3 bell peppers, cut in 1/2 and remove seeds

- 1 diced onion

- 1 15-ounce can of stewed tomatoes

- 1/4 teaspoon of pepper

- 1 pound of ground beef, lean

- 1/2 cup of white rice

- 1/2 teaspoon of onion powder

- 1/2 teaspoon of garlic powder

- 1/2 teaspoon of salt

- 1/2 teaspoon of red pepper flakes

- 1 cup of tomato sauce

- 2 cups of shredded cheddar cheese

- 1 and 1/2 cups of water

- 6 cups of shredded cabbage

Instructions

1. Preheat the Traeger to 325 °F.

2. In a skillet, cook the onions with beef, salt, garlic powder, red pepper flakes, onion powder, salt, and pepper.

3. As the meat is no longer pink, add rice, water, shredded cabbage, stewed tomatoes, and tomato sauce. Cover it and let it simmer until cabbage is soft and rice is cooked.

4. Stuff the bell peppers halves with the beef mix, add cheese on top, and bake for 1/2 an hour.

Chapter 8: Traeger Grill Bonus Recipes

39. Greek Chicken Pizza

(Ready in about: 40 minutes | Serving: 6 | Difficulty: Medium)

Nutrition per serving: Kcal 213 | Fat 11 g | Net Carbs 25 g | Protein 12 g

Ingredients

- 3 tablespoons extra-virgin olive oil

- 3 chicken breasts

- Traeger Fin & Feather rub

- Fresh oregano

- 2 tomatoes, cut into slices

- 1 pizza dough

- 1/4 cup of feta cheese

- 1 cup of fresh spinach

- 2 ounces of Kalamata olives

Instructions

1. Coat chicken with olive oil and season with spice rub.

2. Preheat the Traeger to 375 °F.

3. Put chicken directly on the grate, and cook for 18-20 minutes. Flip and cook until the internal temperature reaches 165 °F.

4. Take chicken out and slice against the grain.

5. Raise Traeger temperature to 400 °F.

6. Roll out pizza dough to your liking. Coat with olive oil and oregano.

7. Put dough directly on the grill. Cook for 3-5 minutes.

8. Take off the grill and add all toppings.

9. Serve hot.

40. Grilled Sweet Potatoes

(Ready in about: 60 minutes | Serving: 12 | Difficulty:

Medium)

Nutrition per serving: Kcal 177 | Fat 8 g | Net Carbs

27 g | Protein 8 g

Ingredients

- 2 yams

- Maple syrup

- 2 sweet potatoes

- 1/2 cup of orange juice

- 1/4 cup of brown sugar bourbon

- 1/2 teaspoon of cinnamon

- 1/2 cup of butter

- 1 teaspoon of salt

Instructions

1. Preheat the grill to 325 °F.

2. Peel yams, potatoes. Cut into rounds (1/4th thick.)

3. In a 10 by 13" oiled baking dish, add layers of potatoes and yams.

4. In a pot, add orange juice, butter, maple syrup on medium flame. Mix until butter melts, for 5 minutes, let it simmer.

5. Turn off the heat.

6. Pour orange/butter sauce over layers of yams and potatoes.

7. Season with cinnamon and salt. Cover with foil.

8. Put on grill cook for 1/2 an hour. Uncover it and cook for 15-30 minutes.

9. Serve hot.

41. Grilled King Crab Legs

(Ready in about: 20 minutes | Serving: 4| Difficulty: Easy)

Nutrition per serving: Kcal 441 | Fat 7 g| Net Carbs 0 g| Protein 88 g

Ingredients

- 1 batch of garlic butter, smoked
- 3-4 pounds of king crab legs

Instructions

1. Preheat the Traeger to 180-200 °F.

2. Split the crab and coat with garlic butter, and place on grill.

3. Smoke for 5 minutes, raise the temperature to 350 to 375 °F.

4. Cook for 5 more minutes, flip and cook for 5 minutes.

5. Serve with garlic butter.

42. Smoked Salmon Scrambled Eggs

(Ready in about: 16 minutes | Serving: 4| Difficulty: Medium)

Nutrition per serving: Kcal 283 | Fat 22 g| Net Carbs 1 g| Protein 19 g

Ingredients

- 1/8 cup of whole milk
- 6 whole eggs
- 1 cup of hot smoked salmon
- 1/4 teaspoon of salt
- 1 tablespoon of salted butter
- A dash of white pepper
- 1 cup of shredded sharp cheddar

Instructions

1. In a bowl, whisk eggs, milk, white pepper, and salt. Mix well.

2. Preheat the Traeger to 350 °F. Place skillet on the grill.

3. In the skillet, melt butter. Add in eggs, cook to set.

4. Add salmon chunks, cheese. Cook until cheese is melted.

5. Serve salmon eggs with the muffins.

43. Grilled Peaches With Yogurt & Granola

(Ready in about: 10 minutes | Serving: 4| Difficulty: Medium)

Nutrition per serving: Kcal 209 | Fat 3 g| Net Carbs 43 g| Protein 6 g

Ingredients

- 1/4 cup of honey
- 4 peaches cut in 1/2
- 1/2 cup of super grains granola
- 1/2 cup of Greek yogurt

Instructions

1. Preheat the Traeger to high.

2. Put peach halves, remove the pit, pit side down, on the grill and cook for 5   minutes

3. Take off the grill and top with yogurt and drizzle honey over.

4. And serve on a bed of granola.

44. Smoked Buffalo Shrimp

(Ready in about: 15 minutes | Serving: 6 | Difficulty: Easy)

Nutrition per serving: Kcal 57 | Fat 1 g | Net Carbs 1 g | Protein 10 g

Ingredients

- 1/4 teaspoon of onion powder

- 1-pound raw shrimp, with tails, peeled and deveined

- 1/4 teaspoon of garlic powder

- 1/2 cup of Buffalo sauce

- 1/2 teaspoon of salt

Instructions

1. Preheat the Traeger to 450 °F.

2. Coat the shrimps with all spices.

3. Place directly on grill cook on each side for 2-3 minutes.

4. Take off the grill coat with buffalo sauce.

5. Serve hot.

45. Traeger Mini Meatloaf Burgers

(Ready in about: 1 hour and 5 minutes | Serving: 12 |

Difficulty: Medium)

Nutrition per serving: Kcal 99 | Fat 5 g | Net Carbs 8

g | Protein 7 g

Ingredients

- 3 pounds of ground beef

- 1 diced onion

- 2 egg yolks

- 1/4 cup of milk

- 1/2 teaspoon of dry mustard

- 3 whole eggs

- 1/2 teaspoon of salt

- 1/2 cup of ketchup

- 1/4 teaspoon of ground black pepper

- 1/2 teaspoon of onion powder

- 1 teaspoon of dried parsley

- 1 tablespoon of minced garlic

- 1 cup of saltine crackers, crushed

- 1/4 teaspoon of garlic powder:

- 1/2 cup of panko breadcrumbs

Instructions

1. Preheat the Traeger to 325 °F.

2. In a bowl, mix all ingredients except for beef.

3. Now add ground beef, mix but do not over mix.

4. Shape into patties and set them aside.

5. Place directly on grates and cook for 10-15 minutes. Brush with BBQ sauce and cook for 5 more minutes until the internal temperature reaches 160 °F.

6. Put cheese on top and melt.

7. Serve hot in buns.

Chapter 9: Dressings & Sauces

46. Sherri Mushroom Sauce

(Ready in about: 20 minutes | Serving: 12 | Difficulty: Easy)

Nutrition per serving: Kcal 33 | Fat 1 g | Net Carbs 4 g | Protein 2 g

Ingredients

- 1 teaspoon of sherry
- 2 cups of milk
- 1 onion, chopped
- 1 and 1/2 cups of sliced fresh mushrooms
- 2 teaspoons of olive oil
- 2 tablespoons of All-purpose flour, plain
- 1 tablespoon of chopped chives
- Salt and black pepper, to taste

Instructions

1. In a pan, heat the milk.

2. In a skillet, sauté onions for 3 minutes in olive oil.

3. Add mushrooms slices and cook for another 3 minutes. Add in the flour and cook for 2-3 minutes.

4. Add in the warmed milk.

5. Continue to stir until it becomes thick, for 3 minutes.

6. Add the rest of the ingredients.

7. Smoke in Traeger for 10 minutes at smoke mode.

8. Serve.

47. Savory Vegetable Dip

(Ready in about: 20 minutes | Serving: 8| Difficulty: Easy)

Nutrition per serving: Kcal 57| Fat 1.5 g| Net Carbs 7 g| Protein 4 g

Ingredients

- 1 cup of fat-free cottage cheese

- 3 cloves of garlic, chopped

- 1/3 cup of plain fat-free yogurt

- 3/4 cup of chopped and sun-dried tomatoes, oil-packed drained

- 1/3 cup of fat-free mayonnaise

Instructions

1. Place all ingredients in the food processor. Pulse until smooth.

2. Smoke in Traeger for 10 minutes at smoke mode.

3. Chill in the refrigerator for 3 hours and serve.

48. Hot Pepper Sauce

(Ready in about: 50 minutes | Serving: 10 | Difficulty: Easy)

Nutrition per serving: Kcal 67 | Fat 2.1 g | Net Carbs 6 g | Protein 0.5 g

Ingredients

- 1/4 cup of olive oil

- 1 ancho chili pepper, dried

- 1 jalapeno chili pepper, fresh

- 1 chipotle chili pepper, dried

- 1/2 cup of water

- 1 cup of white wine vinegar

- 1 New Mexico chili pepper, dried

Instructions

1. Remove stems, seeds from all chilies.

2. In a bowl, mix vinegar and water soak the dried chilies.

3. In a saucepan, add chilies and liquid, add fresh chili.

4. Let it cook for 1/2 an hour. Turn off the heat and let it cool.

5. Blend in a blender until smooth.

6. Smoke in Traeger for 10 minutes at smoke mode.

7. Store in refrigerator.

49. Nut Butter Hummus

(Ready in about: 15 minutes | Serving: 16 | Difficulty: Easy)

Nutrition per serving: Kcal 131 | Fat 4 g | Net Carbs 18 g | Protein 7 g

Ingredients

- 2 cups of garbanzo beans
- 1 cup of water
- 1/2 cup of powdered peanut butter
- 1/4 cup of peanut butter
- 2 tablespoons of honey
- 1 teaspoon of vanilla extract

Instructions

1. In a blender, add all ingredients.

2. Blend until smooth.

3. Smoke in Traeger for 10 minutes at smoke mode.

4. Refrigerate for 1 week.

Conclusion

The Traeger Grill and Smoker grill has functionalities to make it easier for anyone the task of grilling any type of meat or food on the coals. By allowing you to grill, smoke, bake, braise and roast, you will be able to prepare healthier and more appetizing dishes. Those meals that make everyone's mouth water and turn those family gatherings into a memorable moment.

Happiness is associated with a full stomach! That's why we love to share with family and friends those delicious grilled meats that will delight everyone and bring us the best compliments. Be sure to make your favorite people happy with the recipes in this book and always be on the lookout to surprise them with new recipes.

CPSIA information can be obtained
at www.ICGtesting.com
Printed in the USA
BVHW041504180321
602887BV00012B/1659